LUKE

BOOKS OF FAITH SERIES

Learner Session Guide

David L. Tiede

AUGSBURG FORTRESS

Minneapolis

LUKE
Learner Session Guide

Books of Faith Series
Book of Faith Adult Bible Studies

Book of Faith is an initiative of the
Evangelical Lutheran Church in America
God's work. Our hands.

For more information about the Book of Faith initiative, go to www.bookoffaith.org.

References to ELW are from *Evangelical Lutheran Worship* (Augsburg Fortress, 2006).

Web site addresses are provided in this resource for your use. These listings do not represent an endorsement of the sites by Augsburg Fortress, nor do we vouch for their content for the life of this resource.

ISBN: 978-1-4514-0141-7

Writer: David L. Tiede
Cover and interior design: Spunk Design Machine, spkdm.com
Typesetting: Diana M. Running

Manufactured in the U.S.A.
14 13 12 11 1 2 3 4 5 6 7 8 9 10

CONTENTS

Luke 2:1–20

Learner Session Guide

Focus Statement

When Jesus was born, God entered our earthly lives.

Key Verse

To you is born this day in the city of David, a Savior, who is the Messiah, the Lord.
Luke 2:11

Why Was Jesus Born?

Focus Image

He Qi, "Nativity"
Copyright © He Qi. Used by permission.

Gather

Check-in

Take this time to connect or reconnect with the others in your group and give a special welcome for newcomers. Today, we will hear one of the most familiar stories in the Bible, called the "Christmas Gospel." Mary and Joseph were strangers in Bethlehem, where there was "no place for them in the inn" (Luke 2:7). We welcome all as Christ among us!

Pray

Pray or sing these verses from a hymn by Martin Luther.

Welcome to earth, O noble Guest,
through whom this sinful world is blest!
You turned not from our needs away;
how can our thanks such love repay?

For velvets soft and silken stuff
you have but hay and straw so rough
on which as king so rich and great
to be enthroned in humble state.

Notes

Ah, dearest Jesus, holy child,
prepare a bed, soft, undefiled,
a quiet chamber in my heart,
that you and I may never part.
Amen.
("From Heaven Above." *Evangelical Lutheran Worship* 268, verses 8, 11, 12)

Focus Activity

Suppose a non–Christian friend asked you, "Why in the world was Jesus born in a stable?" Using only two minutes, write down the first things you would say.

Open Scripture

Read Luke 2:1–20.

- What words or phrases caught your attention in this familiar story?

- How do you sense God's reign "in the highest heaven" coming to earth?

- How do you imagine the shepherds felt when they returned to their flocks?

Join the Conversation

Literary Context

1. The Gospel according to Luke is famous for its literary beauty, and this story is widely loved, even among people who know very little

Notes

about Jesus or the Christian faith. Although the author's identity is never revealed, the first four verses of the book (Luke 1:1–4) acknowledge that many others have written accounts and emphasize that our author is intent on telling "the truth concerning the things about which you have been instructed."

• Luke 2:1–20 supplies the script that is re-enacted in Christmas pageants in every nation on earth, but this passage isn't only for children. Look again at the lines delivered by the characters in the story. For you, which voices announce the truth of what God is doing here? How do you imagine those voices sounding?

2. Luke's story of Jesus' birth follows wonderful accounts of angelic announcements to Zechariah (Luke 1:13–19) and Mary about God's purposes in the births of John and Jesus (1:28–37). The story also echoes with old scriptural accounts of the birth of Samuel (1 Samuel 1:1—2:10), who anointed David as Israel's king. The Hebrew word for the "anointed one" is *Messiah*, and the Greek word is *Christ*.

• Why is Bethlehem called "the city of David"? See 1 Samuel 16:1-13.

• God took David "from the sheepfolds" where he was tending sheep (Psalm 78:70–72) to anoint him as the shepherd king of Israel. Notice that the angelic messengers explicitly mention "the city of David" as the birthplace of "a savior, who is the Messiah, the Lord" (Luke 2:11). What clues do you get in the story about the kind of king that Jesus will be?

3. Mary plays a powerful role in Luke's story. The angel Gabriel tells her that she will bear this holy child. As God's faithful servant Mary declared, "Let it be with me according to your word" (Luke 1:38). She also prophesied that Jesus would fulfill the promises that God had made to Israel (Luke 1:54–55). Mary was silent in this story, but she "treasured all these words and pondered them in her heart" (Luke 2:19). She would soon hear "a sword will pierce your own soul too" (see Luke 2:35).

• Luke's account of Jesus' birth causes believers and unbelievers to join Mary in wondering, "What in the world will become of this child? How does Mary's response of treasuring and pondering these words prepare you for all that lies ahead in Luke's story of Jesus?

4. With which character or characters do you most closely identify in the story of Jesus' birth? Why?

Notes

Historical Context

1. Note the following places on the map of Palestine in Jesus' time: Nazareth, Galilee, Bethlehem, Judea, and Syria. How far did Joseph and Mary have to travel on their trip from Nazareth to Bethlehem? Imagine taking the journey by foot or on a donkey when about nine months pregnant.

2. Luke regularly alerts the reader to what is happening in the Roman Empire and in the local governance of Roman and Jewish authorities (see Luke 3:1–2; Acts 18:2). Here he mentions the "registration" of the whole empire by Caesar Augustus (probably for taxation and military conscription) and identifies Quirinius as the governor of the Roman province of Syria, which included Galilee and Judea.

• Why do you think information about the Roman emperor and governor are explicitly given in the story?

3. The official Roman messengers proclaimed the "good news" that Caesar was the "savior," and all citizens were required to declare, "Caesar is lord!"

• What do you imagine the Romans might have thought if they heard that God's messengers (the angels) had announced that the "good news" was the birth of Jesus, "a Savior, who is the Messiah, the Lord" (Luke 2:11)?

• Why are those public titles for Jesus still "good news" for our time?

4. Historians believe that by the late first century (when Luke's Gospel was written), the Roman armies had already destroyed Jerusalem, burned the temple, and killed or taken Israel's leaders into slavery.

• In the midst of troubled times when Luke's story was first read, how do you expect the story of Jesus' birth renewed people's hope in God?

• How does the Christmas gospel continue to be especially powerful in times of sorrow or suffering in your family, or in the world? How do suffering people still find hope in this wonderful story?

Lutheran Context

1. Martin Luther compared the Bible to the straw-filled manger that held the Christ child. Lutherans speak of the Bible as the book that reveals Jesus Christ to us. What message about Jesus is "revealed" in this text from Luke? Who has revealed Christ to you most clearly in your life?

2. God's living word speaks both God's law and God's promise, sometimes bringing judgment and again announcing hope. God's word exposes how we have turned away from God, and yet it also reveals God's love and care for us.

• Take a few minutes to think about the past week. What if the angels interrupted your life just as they surprised the shepherds? What would you want to hide from God? What hope would their message give you?

 Notes

Notes

3. Martin Luther was a biblical scholar who understood that the power of the four Gospels lies in their faithfulness to the one gospel that is the good news of what God has done for us in Jesus Christ. Luther wrote:

> Such a story can be told in various ways; one spins it out, the other is brief. Thus, the gospel is and should be nothing else than a chronicle, a story, a narrative about Christ, telling who he is and what he did, said, and suffered—a subject which one describes briefly, another more fully, one this way, another that way." ("Brief Introduction on What to Look for and Expect in the Gospels," Martin Luther's Basic Theological Writings, ed. Timothy Lull. Minneapolis: Augsburg Fortress, 1989, p. 105).

- Read Matthew's story (Matthew 2:1–18) of Jesus' birth. Notice how the cruelty of Herod the Great threatens to overshadow the joy of what God is doing. Both Luke and Matthew are telling the gospel truth of Jesus. Describe how each evangelist opens your heart and mind to understand Jesus' birth.life?

Devotional Context

1. Take another look at the Focus Image on p. 5. How is it similar to or different from other images of Christ's birth? What is most striking to you about this image?

2. We opened our session with verses from Luther's Christmas hymn, "From Heaven Above." It echoes one of the deepest convictions of the Reformation that God has acted to justify and save us. The Gospel story is about how God came to earth among us, and not about our spiritual ascent to God. The Gospel according to John (1:14) declares, "The Word became flesh and lived among us."

- Take a few minutes to reflect on your family's Christmas traditions. Many are good family fun, but some may bring everyone closer to God's intention. Write down one or two ways that observing Christmas could highlight the good news that Jesus' birth means "God is with us."

3. Both Luke and Matthew highlight that Jesus, God in the flesh, was born into a displaced, refugee, or undocumented family.

- Take time to pray for all the work that is done among refugees in the name of Christ by our congregations, Lutheran Social Ministries, Lutheran World Federation, and Lutheran Immigrant and Refugee Services.

- How can you see yourself embodying the good news of Jesus in the world?

Notes

4. People have happy and sad Christmas memories. In the hymn "O Little Town of Bethlehem" we sing, "The hopes and fears of all the years are met in thee tonight!" You already know how the story goes, but as you move together in the coming sessions, listen with Mary and ponder in your heart how God's purposes will unfold in Jesus' life. And how about the unfolding story of your life? Where will Jesus' story meet the hopes and fears of your life?

Wrap-up

Be ready to look back over the work the group has done during the session.

Pray

Lord Jesus, you came as God among us and as an infant in a poor family dislocated by the kingdoms of the world. God's promises for a ruler and Savior all came true in you. You are our Savior and Lord, God who has come among us. Help us be as joyful as the shepherds and join the angels in giving thanks to God. Empower us by your Spirit to tell the world of your love, and give us courage and hope to serve within your reign in this world and the next. We pray in your blessed name, Lord Jesus. Amen.

Extending the Conversation

Homework

1. Read the next session's Bible text: Luke 2:21–40.

2. Take out a manger scene from Christmas storage and put it on your TV, monitor, newspaper, or wherever you get the news of the world. Leave the "wise men" in the box for now, and simply pray the Lord's Prayer for God's kingdom to come on earth as in heaven. With your family or others, discuss how God's kingdom came to earth, and consider what will happen next in Luke's story when the world's rulers find out.

3. Re-read Luke 2:1–20 with special attention to verse 19: "Mary treasured all these words and pondered them in her heart." Which words do you treasure most in the story, and how do you ponder them in your heart and live them?

Notes

Enrichment

1. If you wish to read through the entire book of Luke during this unit, read the following sections this week.

Day 1: Luke 1:1–25

Day 2: Luke 1:26–38

Day 3: Luke 1:39–56

Day 4: Luke 1:57–66

Day 5: Luke 1:67–80

Day 6: Luke 2:1–20

Day 7: Luke 2:21–40

2. Do an Internet search for "images of nativity" or "images of the birth of Jesus." Make note of any images that are especially appealing or interesting to you. You might also consider looking at Christmas scenes from around the world at the following Web site: http://campus.udayton.edu/mary/gallery/creches/crechesworld.html

For Further Reading

The Gospel According to Luke by Michael Patella in New Collegeville Bible Commentary Series (Collegeville, MN: Liturgical Press, 2005). Presents a very accessible commentary to help people read the whole story.

"Session 1: Caesar and Lord" in *Learning Luke: The Apostolic Gospel* by David L. Tiede and friends (selectlearning.org, 2009). A twelve-session video series with study guides on how Luke's story empowers God's mission.

Provoking the Gospel of Luke: A Storyteller's Commentary by Richard W. Swanson (Cleveland: Pilgrim Press, 2006). Provides dramatic clues for presenting the lectionary readings from Luke.

Augsburg Commentary on the New Testament: Luke by David L. Tiede (Minneapolis: Augsburg Fortress, 1988).

Luke 2:21–40

Focus Statement

Every newborn reveals God's love and prompts wonder about the future. The infant Jesus signified that God's promises would be fulfilled, even in the face of opposition.

Key Verse

My eyes have seen your salvation, which you have prepared in the presence of all peoples. Luke 2:30–31

What Will Become of This Child?

Focus Image

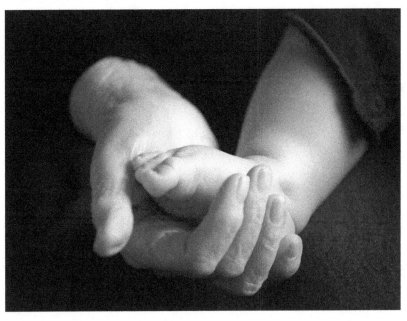

© Design Pics / SuperStock

Gather

Check-in

Take this time to connect or reconnect with the others in your group. Be ready to share new thoughts or insights about your last session. Today, two aged prophets, Simeon and Anna, will open our eyes to see the promise that Jesus will bring into our lives and our world as well as the peril that he will expose.

Pray

Living God, we who are young and we who are old, pray for your Holy Spirit to rest on us. Open our eyes and hearts to see your promises kept in the children you have given us, and may our hope be renewed in the future you brought us through the infant Jesus. Amen.

Focus Activity

Look at the Focus Image. Imagine who is holding the infant, and imagine who the infant is. Then imagine that the older person is asking, "What will become of this child?" Have you ever held a child and asked that question? What hopes and fears lay behind it for you? Share your thoughts with at least one other person.

Notes

Open Scripture

Read Luke 2:21–40.

- How do you imagine Simeon's voice sounded when he praised God for letting him live to see this child who fulfilled God's promises?

- What feelings or emotions do you think different characters may have been feeling in this story?

- What questions are raised for you as you listen to this text?

Join the Conversation

Literary Context

1. This story stands at the center of the first two chapters of Luke's Gospel, introducing Luke's whole narrative. Both Simeon and Anna speak prophetically in this story, and Anna is explicitly called a prophet. Prophecy often includes an element of prediction, but the primary force of prophetic speech is the announcement of God's word and will. Look closely at 2:25–28.

- What clue does Luke give about Simeon that helps us know that what he says about Jesus in 2:29–32 is true?
- How are his words similar to those of the angel in 2:10–11?

2. Notice how Simeon's first words (2:29–32) are all in praise or blessing of God for God's faithfulness to the salvation promised by the prophets. He is speaking of Jesus. To what people will Jesus be a "light"? To what people is he given for their "glory"? As you look forward to Luke's whole story, what do you think this will mean?

3. Simeon's second prophetic message, spoken as a blessing of Mary and Joseph, is surprisingly harsh. Now we know that God knows Jesus' mission is not going to be easy. Jesus will expose human defiance of God's will. As the plot of Luke's story moves forward with Jesus bringing God's reign on earth, what sort of resistance, refusal, and rejection will he encounter? Who will resist him? What will God do then?

4. Notice the sequence when Simeon announces 1) "the falling" and 2) "the rising of many in Israel." This is not a story of the rise and fall of an empire, but a prophetic diagnosis of how even after many of God's people have stumbled and fallen, God will bring about a rising. What word does the prophet Anna use to describe this "rising" (2:38)? What does that word mean for you??

Historical Context

1. This is one of Luke's many scenes in the Jerusalem temple. The temple was more than a large church building, even more than a national cathedral. It was understood as the dwelling place of God, where God's hovering presence assured the nation's safety. Even the Romans usually stayed away from its most holy precincts. By the time Luke's Gospel was written, the Roman conquest of Jerusalem in 70 CE was probably a painful memory, etched with accounts of the slaughter of the priests at the altar.

• Notice how Simeon was "looking forward to the consolation of Israel" and Anna joined those "who were looking for the redemption of Jerusalem." Christians rightly observe that Jesus was not merely "a political messiah," but were Simeon and Anna's hopes fulfilled? Do you think God's promises failed when the Romans destroyed Jerusalem? How is Jesus a sign of hope even when the forces of evil appear to triumph?

2. Notice how when Mary and Joseph "had finished everything required by the law of the Lord," they returned to Nazareth. Joseph, Mary, Simeon, and Anna were all faithful to God's law, and Jesus was born in Judea and raised in Galilee.

• Some Christian commentaries on Luke call it the "Gentile Gospel." Luke makes fewer references than Matthew to Hebrew or Aramaic words, and the scriptures that Luke read were probably written in Greek, but the story is still about Israel. The word *Gentile* means "nations." What do you think it means that the glory of God's chosen people is—and has always been—to be a light to the nations of the world?

 Notes

Notes

Lutheran Context

1. Martin Luther was an Old Testament scholar. His commentaries on Genesis and the Psalms illustrate that he was deeply aware of the living God. His interpretations of the New Testament are filled with Israel's Scriptures. Thus, the Book of Faith is also about the whole Bible, and Simeon and Anna are almost Old Testament characters because their appearances took place when Jesus had not yet been anointed for his mission. They embody Israel's best faith: confident of God's promises, now welcoming the infant Messiah, and deeply aware that this child will face hard things.

- How do Simeon and Anna inspire you to trust God's promises, even though you may not see the complete fulfillment of those promises in your lifetime?

- Have you wondered why parents and grandparents often have tears in their eyes when they bring their infants for baptism? How are their hopes and fears like those of Anna or Simeon?

2. Lutheran Christians are aware that sin is turning away from God or even opposing God. Even as we seek to trust in God's mercy, we are still caught in our own schemes, self-interests, and sin, so that we find ourselves resisting or defying God, even when we want to do better. We yearn for the purity of heart to welcome Christ Jesus into our lives, yet we also realize that we benefit from economic and political systems that may guard our privileges more than they protect the vulnerable who live among us.

- If Christ Jesus appeared in the here and now of your community, so that "the inner thoughts of many [would] be revealed" (2:35), what personal or public parts of your life or your community do you think people would not want him to see?

3. In his explanation of the third article of the Apostles' Creed in the Small Catechism, Martin Luther speaks of the Holy Spirit as the one who "has called me through the gospel, enlightened me with his gifts, made me holy, and kept me in the true faith . . ." As you look back at the role of the Holy Spirit in this text, how does this definition of the Holy Spirit seem to fit? In what way does the Spirit call to you through the message of this passage?

Devotional Context

1. Simeon's praise of God has been rehearsed throughout Christian history. The Latin phrase *Nunc dimittis* means "Now you are dismissing," We often sing Simeon's song as we depart from the Lord's Supper. In some Christian communities, such as certain places in China, people often weep as they leave the Lord's table.

- Discuss why it is that faithful people can be so moved by what they have seen, heard, and tasted in the Lord's Supper.
- Have you ever been deeply touched with a sense of God's presence?

2. Simeon's song is regularly sung in funerals for elderly Christians. Ancient Christian artists often depicted Simeon with tears flowing from his physically blind eyes. They believed that when he said, "My eyes have seen your salvation," he "saw" with the eyes of his trusting heart, just as elderly people often die trusting promises they will not "see."

- When have you experienced the profound witness of this song?
- How has the faith of someone who has died helped you to trust God in your life?

3. What do you suppose Mary was feeling when Simeon declared that Jesus would be a "sign that will be opposed" and that "a sword will piece [Mary's] own soul too"? If you are a parent, when have you experienced concern or fear over what may lie ahead for your child? What helps you to face those fears?

4. How can Christ's followers continue Israel's calling, or vocation, to be a light to the nations?

Wrap–up

Be ready to look back over the work your group has done in this session.

Pray

O Lord, now let your servant depart in heav'nly peace,
for I have seen the glory of your redeeming grace:
a light to lead the nations unto your holy hill,
the glory of your people, your chosen Israel.

Then grant that I may follow your gleam, O glorious Light,
till earthly shadows scatter, and faith is changed to sight;
till raptured saints shall gather upon that shining shore,
where Christ, the blessed daystar, shall light them evermore.
("O Lord, Now Let Your Servant Depart in Heav'nly Peace," ELW 313)

Extending the Conversation

Homework

1. Read the next session's Bible text: Luke 4:14–30.

2. Many congregations observe the practice of giving a candle for families to light on the anniversary of a baptism. They usually refer to

 Notes

Notes

Jesus' words in Matthew 5:14–16: "You are the light of the world . . . let your light shine before others, so that they may see your good works and give glory to your Father in heaven." Write down the names of a) a person who was recently baptized; b) someone who was baptized many years ago; and c) yourself. Light a candle and pray for the light of Christ to shine in those lives and in the lives of all the baptized to the glory of God.

3. Reread Simeon's blessing of Jesus' mother and father and his dire warning to Mary (Luke 2:34–35). From what you already know about the story, imagine the times when Mary's soul was pierced by what happened to Jesus. How does Simeon's prophecy prepare us for what is coming?

Enrichment

1. If you wish to read through the entire book of Luke during this unit, read the following sections this week.

Day 1: Luke 2:41–52

Day 2: Luke 3:1–6

Day 3: Luke 3:7–14

Day 4: Luke 3:15–20

Day 5: Luke 3:21–38

Day 6: Luke 4:1–13

Day 7: Luke 4:14–30

For Further Reading

The Gospel According to Luke by Michael Patella in New Collegeville Bible Commentary Series (Collegeville, MN: Liturgical Press, 2005), pp. 19–22.

"Session 2: Prophecy and History" in *Learning Luke: The Apostolic Gospel* by David L. Tiede and friends (selectlearning.org).

Provoking the Gospel of Luke: A Storyteller's Commentary by Richard W. Swanson (Cleveland: Pilgrim Press, 2006), pp. 97-100.

Augsburg Commentary on the New Testament: Luke by David L. Tiede (Minneapolis: Augsburg Fortress, 1988), pp. 72-79.

"Introduction to Luke" in *Lutheran Study Bible* by Richard W. Swanson (Minneapolis: Augsburg Fortress, 2009), pp. 1694-1695.

Luke 4:14–30

Learner Session Guide

Focus Statement

Today is God's time!

Key Verse

Today this scripture has been fulfilled in your hearing!
Luke 4:21

Let God Be God!

Focus Image

© Ikon Images / SuperStock

Gather

Check–in

Greet each other as those about to hear Jesus' inaugural address. Treat each other as the assembly of the people in Nazareth: farmers, fishermen, mothers, elderly, and young. Or welcome each other as platform guests at a presidential inauguration. Jesus is about to announce God's reign. What would the world look like if we enacted Jesus' program?

Pray

Lord Jesus, you have come among us in the majesty of God's mercy and justice. We are hopeful for your reign among us and eager to hear your word for us. To tell the truth, we are also worried about all you may have in mind. We often prefer that you would just bless what we have going, confirming our special place in God's family. But we know you have larger plans for the world, greater love for our neighbors, and costly calls to us. We pray, therefore, for your Holy Spirit to open our hearts, our minds, and our lives to hear, obey, and enact your will in all that we say and do. In your name, we pray. Amen.

Notes

Focus Activity

At the top of a sheet of paper, write, "Jesus is Lord!" Then draw a vertical line down the center of the page. Put a plus sign at the top of the left column and a minus sign on the right. Why are you glad and what makes you uneasy that Jesus is Lord? In what way is this confession a "plus" (left)? In what way might it be a "minus" (right)? Write one or two thoughts on each side of the line. Share your thoughts with one or two others in your group.

Open Scripture

Read Luke 4:14–30.

- What did you hear in Jesus' words that inspired you?

- What did Jesus say or do that made you uncomfortable?

- Why do you suppose the people became so angry?

Join the Conversation

Literary Context

1. Luke is sometimes called "The Holy Spirit Gospel," and the book of Acts is often called "The Acts of the Holy Spirit." The writer, sometimes called the evangelist, set the stage for the beginning of Jesus' ministry in Nazareth by frequent references to the Holy Spirit. We saw that three times in the story of Simeon in our previous session (Luke 2:25–35). Take a pencil and underline the words "Holy Spirit" or "Spirit" in the following texts:

- Luke 3:21–22; Acts 10:38 (Jesus' is baptized.)
- Luke 4:1–13 (Jesus is tempted by the devil.)
- Luke 4:14–16 (Jesus' ministry begins in Galilee.)

In your own words, describe what you see God doing in the story.

2. Take time to appreciate how carefully the scene is set for Jesus' very brief message. Read the following condensed version of the story to focus on all of Jesus' actions, zeroing in on Isaiah's prophecy, centering on Jesus' word:

READER #1: Then Jesus, filled with the power of the Spirit, returned to Galilee.

READER #2: He began to teach in their synagogues. He went to the synagogue on the Sabbath day.

READER #3: He stood up to read.

READER #4: He unrolled the scroll and found the place where it was written:

ALL: The Spirit of the Lord is upon me, because he has anointed me to bring good news to the poor. He has sent me to proclaim release to the captives and recovery of sight to the blind, to let the oppressed go free, to proclaim the year of the Lord's favor.

READER #4: He rolled up the scroll and gave it back to the attendant.

READER #3: And sat down.

READER #2: The eyes of all in the synagogue were fixed on him.

READER #1: Then he began to say to them:

ALL: Today this scripture has been fulfilled in your hearing.

• Notice that Jesus' whole sermon on Isaiah's text was just one sentence long! What is so promising about God's word in the Isaiah prophecy? What would people say if Jesus announced this message to your community, "Today it all happens!"?

3. Note the second half of the story when the people reject Jesus' message. After they said, "Is not this Joseph's son?" (4:22), Jesus apparently saw they had already rejected him and his mission from God. Read 4:23–27 carefully. What words or phrases seem to cause the crowd to turn angry? How would you feel if Jesus spoke like that in your congregation?

Historical Context

1. Luke's Gospel and the book of Acts give us rare glimpses into the synagogues of the first century. Historians and archeologists who study Jewish history have documented a wide variety of these local "houses of prayer" and "houses of study" from earlier centuries when the people of Israel were first "scattered" in Babylonia and Egypt (in the diaspora), and then through the times of the Greek and Roman Empires. While the temple was standing in Jerusalem, the synagogues in Judea and Galilee housed the local communities of faith for people in Judea and Galilee.

 Notes

Notes

• Notice that Jesus "stood up to read" and "sat down" to speak. Imagine your church with no seating for the people. How would that feel different from most churches where preachers stand to speak while the people sit?

2. Imagine reading the book of Isaiah in the form of a scroll. The "book" with pages sewn together on a spine did not become standard until centuries after the time of Jesus. The synagogue in Nazareth probably owned hand copied scrolls on sheepskin of the first five "books of Moses" (also known as the law or Torah) and of some prophets and writings. These scrolls were treasures, probably kept in clay jars or secure wooden boxes.

• What if the pastor had to unroll a long scroll to find a passage from Isaiah? Would the scriptures seem more "holy" if they were on scrolls? How would that affect the way you'd listen if you couldn't read the Bible on your own?

• What if the only copies of the Bible were handwritten? Before the printing press and the Reformation, most people only heard the Bible read in worship, and often in Latin, which few people could understand. How do you experience the power of Isaiah's prophetic words when you hear them in the music of Handel's Messiah or as a direct address to you?

2. In Luke 4:19, Jesus is reading Isaiah's announcement of "the year of the Lord's favor." This is the "year of jubilee" and restoration promised in Leviticus 25:8–12. It meant debt forgiveness and restoration of land to those who had lost it in debt.

• Imagine a rural community where owning land is the economic backbone for families. Who would be glad and who would be unhappy if a "jubilee" were announced, giving land back to those whose property had been foreclosed?

Lutheran Context

1. The prophets knew that God had made their words "like a sharp sword" (Isaiah 49:2), cutting through human pretenses with both liberation for the oppressed and judgment on the oppressors. Luther emphasized that God's word communicates both God's commands and God's promises. God's law shines a light on our sins and self-interest just when we think we have hidden them in our achievements. Even God's promises disrupt the status quo, and we may be offended when we think we are entitled to our well-being. Such truth telling can also be "good news" for those who have been harmed by our self-righteousness.

• It is easy to criticize the people in Nazareth for rejecting Jesus, but what if you take Isaiah's promises literally, as personally addressed to you? Draw a picture of your face as you are hearing all of Jesus'

Notes

words. You don't need to show the picture to anyone. When are you smiling and when are you wincing?

- How are Isaiah's words spoken by Jesus "good news" to you? Who might hear these words as the best news possible?

2. "Let God be God!" was one of the great watchwords of the Reformation, but that is not an easy instruction to follow. Most of the time, we are focused on our own schemes to get ahead and to be in control. Even congregations and denominations get stuck on achieving their own success when the world around them cries out in need. Jesus' sermon in Nazareth was and is a wake-up call to God's agenda for those in need.

- Recall a time when your congregation paid more attention to people in need than to preserving itself. How was that experience threatening, and how was it liberating for the congregation?

Devotional Context

1. Look back to the Focus Image on page 19. What do you think is happening in the scene? How does the use of color affect the way you interpret this illustration? Have you ever had to speak to a hostile crowd? Have you ever had to take a stand for something against the majority? How is being a follower of Jesus sometimes a "minority" position?

2. Almost three centuries ago, Johannes Albrecht Bengel wrote:
> *"Apply yourself totally to the text.*
> *Apply the text totally to yourself."*

Understanding the Bible is the beginning of letting the word of Christ dwell in you richly (Colossians 3:16). Take time to dwell in this story, to savor, to appreciate, to meditate on the calling that God has for you as you follow Jesus in your home and family, your workplace, your public life, and your congregation. Write down some thoughts about this, and share them with another person in the group.

3. The bold vision for the Book of Faith initiative is:

That the whole church become more fluent in the first language of faith, the language of Scripture, in order that we might live into our calling as a people renewed, enlivened, empowered, and sent by the Word.

- Discuss this question with two other people: How does this story help you discern the calling and commission that God is giving your congregation, to be sent by Jesus into the world?

Notes

Wrap-up

Be ready to look back over the work your group has done in this session.

Pray

Almighty and ever-living God, increase in us the gifts of faith, hope, and love; and that we may obtain what you promise, make us love what you command, through your Son, Jesus Christ, our Savior and Lord. Amen. (Collect for the fourth Sunday after Epiphany, ELW, p. 23)

Extending the Conversation

Homework

1. Read the next session's Bible text: Luke 7:1–17.

2. Consider compiling a WWJD (What Would Jesus Do?) scrapbook. Week by week, as you are reading through Luke's Gospel, make clippings from the newspaper or magazines, insert photos from family and community events, and leave room for your own comments. In the light of what Jesus said he was about to do and what he ultimately did in his mission, what would he do about these things?

3. Explore the Old Testament stories that Jesus refers to in today's text: Elijah in Sidon (1 Kings 17:1–16) and Elisha and the Syrian (2 Kings 5:1–14). Those stories also provide biblical precedent for what Jesus does in Luke 7:1–17 (see the next session).

Enrichment

1. If you wish to read through the entire book of Luke during this unit, read the following sections this week.

> Day 1: Luke 4:31-44
>
> Day 2: Luke 5:1-11
>
> Day 3: Luke 5:12-26
>
> Day 4: Luke 5:27-39
>
> Day 5: Luke 6:1-11
>
> Day 6: Luke 6:12-19
>
> Day 7: Luke 6:20-49

2. Internet Web sites present varied interpretations of the year of Jubilee. Wikipedia can link you to both Jewish and Christian resources, such as Roman Catholic traditions of pilgrimage and several American Evangelical traditions of personal renewal. For a "Jubilee" critique of the tyranny of debt in impoverished countries, see www.jubileeusa.org.

For Further Reading

The Gospel According to Luke by Michael Patella in New Collegeville Bible Commentary Series (Collegeville, MN: Liturgical Press, 2005), pp. 23–31.

"Session 3: Jesus Goes Public" in *Learning Luke: The Apostolic Gospel* by David L. Tiede and friends (selectlearning.org).

Provoking the Gospel of Luke: A Storyteller's Commentary by Richard W. Swanson (Cleveland: Pilgrim Press, 2006), pp. 90–97.

Augsburg Commentary on the New Testament: Luke by David L. Tiede (Minneapolis: Augsburg Fortress, 1988). pp. 101–111.

Notes

Luke 7:1–17

Learner Session Guide

Focus Statement

Jesus embodies God's authority and enacts God's compassion.

Key Verse

A great prophet has risen among us! God has looked favorably on his people!
Luke 7:16

What Was Jesus Doing?

Focus Image

The Sick Waiting for Jesus to Pass
James Tissot (1836–1902 French)
© SuperStock / SuperStock

Gather

Check–in

As you arrive today, take time to think about anyone you know who is ill, or who may have recently died. Consider bringing that person's name and/or the family before the Lord in prayer.

Pray

Almighty God, you inspired your servant Luke to reveal in his gospel the love and healing power of your Son. Give your church the same love and power to heal, and to proclaim your salvation among the nations to the glory of your name, through Jesus Christ, your Son, our healer, who lives and reigns with you and the Holy Spirit, one God, now and forever. Amen.
(Collect for the day of Luke, Evangelist, October 18, ELW, p. 58)

Focus Activity

Look at the Focus Image titled The Sick Waiting for Jesus to Pass. What kinds of illnesses or physical challenges do you imagine some of the people by the road are experiencing? Have you or someone close to you ever waited for, hoped for healing? Are you or this other person still waiting?

In the story of the centurion, the officer interceded for his servant. In the story of the widow of Nain, Jesus was deeply moved by the death of the widow's son. Knowing our Lord's compassion for all who suffer and confident in the great resurrection of all who belong to Christ Jesus, pray now for God's healing and love for someone who is ill or in need of comfort.

Open Scripture
Read Luke 7:1–17.

- What images in these stories of healing stand out to you? Why?

- What questions do these stories raise as you listen to them?

- With which character do you most closely identify?

Notes

Join the Conversation

Literary Context

1. The story of the healing of the centurion's servant follows Jesus' "Sermon on the Plain" (6:17–49), and Luke introduces a new section of the narrative by reporting that "after Jesus had finished all his sayings he entered Capernaum" (7:1). The Messiah has been announcing his program, and now he will show his prophetic compassion as Messiah. In this part of the story, Jesus will be well-received and will not encounter rejection.

- In the first scene, notice the relationship between the Jewish elders and the Roman centurion. What surprising thing has the centurion done for his Jewish neighbors?

- The centurion displays what military personnel call "the habit of command." He knows how to give orders and he knows when he is outranked. How does that come out when Jesus comes near to the centurion's house? What is Jesus' reaction?

Notes

2. Compare this story in Luke's Gospel to Matthew's version (see Matthew 8:5–13). What differences do you see? What role does faith play in each?

3. Jesus' compassion for the widow reveals him to be a Messiah with heart. Notice how he breaks into the funeral and crosses the boundaries of clean and unclean by walking up and touching the cot on which they were carrying the corpse. Tell a story of a time when you have seen a person of authority set it all aside because he or she was moved by someone's suffering.

4. In Luke's narrative, the message that God will "visit [God's] people" (or as it is translated in the NRSV, "look favorably on [God's] people") is sounded hopefully in Zechariah's song in Luke 1:68, and later resounds with Jesus' judgment as he approached Jerusalem ("because you did not recognize the time of your visitation from God." Luke 19:44).

- Recall a time when you were aware that God was with you to protect, heal, or guide you. Something more than good luck was with you. Maybe like the people in Nain, you even said (aloud or under your breath), "Thank God!" In the story of your life, what did you do next?

Historical Context

1. The centurion was an officer in the army of Roman occupation. Like the centurion in a different story whom Peter visited when directed by a heavenly vision (Acts 10:1–48), this officer was not an Israelite but was known as a friend of Israel. Many parts of Luke's Gospel involve outsiders who are more faithful than the insiders.

- Draw a picture of someone you know or know about who understood Jesus and his mission when people inside the church lagged behind.
- Watch the newspaper for a story of military service personnel who show forth the love of Christ in places where nationals resent them as occupiers.

2. Jewish tradition has long been very careful about burial practices, and Christians have continued that respect. Biblical faith, however, knows a power greater than death. In Nain, Jesus enacted the prophetic faith that God's love is stronger than death.

- Many people grieve their sons and daughters who have gone to early graves because of accidents, violence, or disease. Jesus doesn't interrupt those services. How does this story help you envision Jesus' authority, even over death?

Lutheran Context

1. One of the deep Lutheran convictions about the Bible is that scripture itself often gives the best interpretation of scripture because it is all God's story and action. That is why we also read scripture as a mirror to make sense of our own lives. Sometimes, interpretation of scripture by the scripture happens directly, as when Jesus declared Isaiah's prophecy as fulfilled in Nazareth (Luke 4:21) and where he cited the prophetic precedents of Elijah and Elisha in Luke 4:25-27. But Jesus often enacted or re-enacted God's story in scripture without specifically saying it.

Jesus' healing of the centurion's son reminds us of Elisha's healing of the foreign army commander Naaman in 2 Kings (5:1-19), and Jesus' raising in Nain is almost a replay of Elijah's raising of a widow's son in 1 Kings (17:17-24).

- Compare the stories from 1 Kings and 2 Kings with the stories in today's text from Luke. How do those Old Testament stories help shed light on the meaning of the New Testament stories in Luke? How is God at work in each?

2. Both stories from the Old Testament conclude when the great prophet "gave him to his mother." That is not mere coincidence or an accident of history, because God who has long been full of compassion for widows and orphans is still at work.

- Take time to listen to one another. Who has experienced this kind of divine care in a time of need? What stories have you heard about such love from God? How does reading these Bible stories help you to sense God among us?

3. Maybe some of those in great need around you are actually widows or parents who have lost children. Maybe you know young people who have been lost to drugs or prostitution. Take some time with local school personnel, police, and social service agencies to identify who is at the greatest risk in your community. Then ask yourself, "What was Jesus doing with the widow and her son? What would Jesus do now, and for whom?"

Devotional Context

1. These two stories offer glimpses of God's compassion. The prophets of Israel were swept into the anguish of God's love. The God of the Bible is not detached or living in the clouds. Biblical prophecy is alive with divine pathos. In Jesus, God came to earth, touched by human suffering and pained by human indifference.

- What words do you think Jesus the Messiah has for those who do not experience physical healing in response to their prayers for help?

 Notes

Notes

• How do you see the stories of Jesus the Healer as both promising and potentially painful?

2. Draw one picture of Jesus healing the servant of this foreign soldier and another picture of him taking on death itself on behalf of the widow. If possible, draw the faces of participants in this study on the crowds of amazed people as they declare: "A great prophet has risen among us! God has looked favorably on his people." (Luke 7:16)

3. Sometimes, we do not ask for healing help because we feel unworthy to receive it. What would it take for you to feel "worthy" to have Jesus come to your aid?

4. What would it mean for Jesus to "visit" your congregation? What healing do you hope he would bring?

Wrap-up

Be ready to look back over the work your group has done in this session.

Pray

Come, Lord Jesus, be our guest,
And may the world you love be blessed.
Messiah and Prophet of compassion,
Draw near to us and us to you,
That we may live your resurrection. Amen.

Extending the Conversation

Homework

1. Read the next session's Bible text: Luke 9:18–36.

2. Visit someone who is homebound or in the hospital. Find out if the individual knows that people are praying for him or her. Invite that person to tell you how he or she remains confident that God is with him or her, even at times when friends and family are not present.

3. Call the family of someone in your community who is serving in the military. Let the family know that they have your prayerful support, and ask for a photo of their loved one so that you can pray for that person by name. Reach out in this way to more than one family, if possible.

Enrichment

1. If you wish to read through the entire book of Luke during this unit, read the following sections this week.

Day 1: Luke 7:18–35

Day 2: Luke 7:36–50

Day 3: Luke 8:1–18

Day 4: Luke 8:19–25

Day 5: Luke 8:26–39

Day 6: Luke 8:40–56

Day 7: Luke 9: 1–17

2. Lutheran Services in America is an umbrella organization for a wide variety of Lutheran social ministries. From the time of the immigration of Lutherans into North America through the eras of relocating refugees after every war, Lutherans have simply known that God has called us to serve our neighbors, whether they are Lutheran or Christian or not. In the past two centuries, Lutherans have developed the largest faith-based network of social ministries in North America. Visit the Web site of Lutheran Services in America to report on the range and complexity of this work. Serving our neighbors started with Jesus in stories like those in chapter 7 of Luke.

3. Lutherans have also been industry leaders in the development of hospital and medical care for disease and trauma. The economics and public policies of twenty-first century health care have made it more difficult to sustain the Christian identity of hospital systems that were once vigorously Lutheran. Still, almost every community and congregation includes people whose occupations in health care are profound vocations for them. If your congregation has a parish nurse or includes physicians or other health care providers, ask one of the learners to interview one of those professionals to explore this question: "How is your work a fulfillment of Jesus' ministry of healing?"

 Notes

Notes

For Further Reading

The Gospel According to Luke by Michael Patella in New Collegeville Bible Commentary Series (Collegeville, MN: Liturgical Press, 2005), pp. 47–50.

"Session 4: Messiah and Prophet" in *Learning Luke: The Apostolic Gospel* by David L. Tiede and friends (selectlearning.org).

Provoking the Gospel of Luke: A Storyteller's Commentary by Richard W. Swanson (Cleveland: Pilgrim Press, 2006).

Augsburg Commentary on the New Testament: Luke by David L. Tiede (Minneapolis: Augsburg Fortress, 1988), pp. 147–159.

Learner Session Guide

Focus Statement

Jesus leads us into great challenges.

Key Verse

This is my Son, my Chosen; listen to him! Luke 9:35

Why Must Jesus Die?

Focus Image

© Flirt / SuperStock

Gather

Check-in

Take this time to connect or reconnect with the others in your group. Be ready to share new thoughts or insights about your last session.

Pray

Lord Jesus, you have called us to follow you as your disciples, and you have sent us into the world to be your apostles among all those people you love, even those who despise you. You never promised it would be easy, but you went before us with courage, vision, and determination, even to your death, which you saw coming. We pray today to be caught up in your mission, unafraid to follow you and confident of your love for us. Amen.

Focus Activity

Take a close look at the Focus Image. What do you imagine has happened/is happening? What do you think the rescuer is feeling? Have you ever been in a desperate rescue situation, either as the one being rescued or as the one doing the rescuing? Do you know someone whose work involves serving in dangerous situations?

Notes

Open Scripture
Read Luke 9:18–36.

- What words or actions caught your attention in these verses?

- How do Jesus' words about following him make you feel?

- What was most awesome to you about Jesus' transfiguration?

Join the Conversation

Literary Context

We are at the point in the story when Jesus is completing a major phase of teaching, with demonstrations of who he is as Messiah and Prophet of God. Shortly after the end of our reading for this session, Jesus will "set his face to go to Jerusalem," and the Samaritans will not receive him "because his face was set toward Jerusalem" (9:51–53).

The question "Who is Jesus?" leads us with Jesus' disciples to other questions that fill us with concern: "Who are we?" "What does it mean to follow Jesus?" We are drawn into the story with both hope and fear. In the light of Jesus' transfiguration, we sense that Jesus is on a path to unavoidable conflict, suffering, and death. Why must Jesus die? Our fear, "What will become of us?" is illumined by our faith that through difficulties and even death, God's reign is coming. As Paul and Barnabas later encouraged the disciples in Antioch, "It is through many persecutions that we must enter the kingdom of God" (Acts 14:22).

1. Our story follows Jesus' authorization of the mission of the twelve disciples and the intimidating question from Herod, who asks, "Who

Notes

is this about whom I hear such things?" Read Luke 9:1–6 and Luke 9:7–9.

• Compare the sending of the twelve in Luke 9:1–6 with the sending of the seventy in 10:1–12. How are the disciples told to travel? The ancient world was well acquainted with traveling hucksters and religious scams. When have you seen someone representing Jesus with the integrity of simplicity?

2. Peek ahead to Luke 13:31–33 to see how Herod's threat escalates to the point that he wants to kill Jesus. Herod will appear again in Jesus' trial in Jerusalem. Think of one or more other tyrants who first became an adversary and then the executioner of a righteous person. Why did that person take that path?

3. The glory of God shines forth with words of acclamation for Jesus from the cloud. This story is told in close agreement with Mark 9:2–10 and Matthew 17:1–9, but only Luke includes the rich details about how Moses and Elijah were "speaking of [Jesus'] departure, which he was about to accomplish in Jerusalem" (Luke 9:31–33). The Greek word for "departure" is *exodus*, like the name of the Old Testament book of Exodus that tells the story of Israel's miraculous departure, or exodus, from Egypt.

• Imagine how the message of Jesus' accomplishing a departure/exodus would have sounded to Simeon and Anna who were "looking forward to the consolation of Israel" and "looking for the redemption of Jerusalem" (Luke 2:25,38). Can you feel the hope growing even as the threat rises?

4. The story of the Transfiguration is the concluding Gospel lesson in the Epiphany season of the church year, and it is followed by Ash Wednesday and Lent. Many readers have sensed that this story is a preview of the accounts of Jesus' resurrection. The concluding sentence reads: "And they kept silent and in those days told no one any of the things they had seen" (Luke 9:36).

• Why do you think the disciples chose to be silent about this experience? In what way do you consider the transfiguration and resurrection of Jesus to be similar?

Historical Context

As we hear "the greatest story ever told" about Jesus' ministry and mission, we need to remember that the evangelists wrote about events that actually happened. Writing forty to fifty years after Jesus' life, death, and resurrection, they were retelling the stories that "eyewitnesses and servants of the word" (Luke 1:2) had chosen to tell in both oral and written forms. They had seen God's Messiah at

Notes

work. At this point in Luke's account, the disciples see God at work in Jesus, but they don't understand why Jesus is about to lead them into profound danger, even death—his and theirs. Luke takes us inside this historical power struggle, confident that Jesus knew what was happening, without trite answers as to why all of the impending danger must come before Jesus' triumph.

1. Take a pencil and underline the following speakers in today's text. What name or names for Jesus are used by each of these?
    a. The crowds (9:19)
    b. Peter (9:20)
    c. Jesus (9:22 and 26)
    d. God (9:35)

• How dangerous do you suppose any of those titles would be to Jesus and his followers if a client king of the Romans, such as Herod, or a procurator, such as Pilate, even got wind of a rumor that John the Baptist or Elijah or an ancient prophet had come to life? Who might react most strongly if the word got out that Jesus' followers believed him to be God's Messiah?

• Even the title "Son of Man" that Jesus used was loaded with power. To explore this further, look up Ezekiel 2:1-8 where God sends the son of man with a message of judgment (NRSV translated as "mortal") or see the "son of man" as name for the judge God sends at the end of time (see Daniel 7:13).

2. Martin Luther King's "I Have a Dream" speech includes the specific warning to his followers, "I may not get there with you!" as well as his affirmations that he would also prefer a long life without troubles. He was enacting his understanding of the script of Jesus' journey into the perils of Jerusalem. What sense does it make to you that Martin Luther King sustained his hope in the dream amid real danger? What other big dreams can you think of that were realized only in the face of grave danger?

Lutheran Context

1. Many ancient and modern people who are inspired by Jesus don't like the harsh realities in the Gospel stories, preferring a more "spiritual" vision of Jesus. The ancient "Gnostic" gospels are filled with accounts of Jesus' mysterious sayings and miraculous powers, but they mention almost nothing about his death. The media often hail those versions as more "enlightened" for aiding human "spirituality." Why do you think the cross is offensive to some who want a more "spiritual" Jesus?

Notes

2. All four Gospels in the Bible, however, are emphatic about Jesus' marching directly into harm's way in Jerusalem, and they devote large portions of their narratives to Jesus' trial and execution. This is not a story of how humans rose to new spiritual heights but of how God came to the earth to reach us in the flesh. What difference does it make that our salvation or redemption is based on what God "has done," rather than on what we "do"?

3. Martin Luther spoke of "the theology of the cross" as the Christian honesty to call things what they truly are without glossing over pain and suffering, rejecting a "theology of glory" which denies the reality of evil. God's glory is revealed amid the depths of resistance and violence, not to glorify the violence or suffering, but to "accomplish the exodus," that is, to liberate us from sin, death, and the power of evil.

- An "exodus" is a liberation or a departure from bondage to freedom. Such a rescue often requires great sacrifice from the liberators. Tell a story of a costly rescue operation, perhaps by police or firefighters, maybe by military personnel, or perhaps from your family history. Why were the rescuers willing to take risks and make sacrifices?

4. Moses and Elijah may represent "the law and the prophets" bearing witness to Jesus in the story. Remember that God appeared to each of them in the clouds on a mountain and both had dramatic "departures" at the end of their lives. Notice that the "voice from the cloud" pronounces about Jesus, "This is my Son, my Chosen," while at his baptism, the voice from heaven addressed Jesus directly, "You are my Son, the Beloved" (3:22).

- Have you (or has someone you know) experienced God's presence in some dramatic way? Was it like the stories in the Bible? Why do you suppose God is partially hidden in a cloud that only God's voice is heard?

Devotional Context

1. The hymn "Son of God, Eternal Savior" (ELW 655) expresses our deep awe for how Jesus enacted God's reign of mercy. Our scripture story reveals that Jesus knew how costly that grace was going to be. God's words from the cloud to Moses, to Elijah, and to Jesus draw us into God's purposes and calling.

- Consider what it means to be God's "Chosen" one. God's voice says, "Listen to him!" What do you expect to hear as Jesus moves forward?

Notes

• In *Fiddler on the Roof*, Tevye laments, "God, I know we are the chosen people. But once in a while, can't you choose someone else?" Think about the suffering love of such great saints as Mother Teresa or Dietrich Bonhoeffer. Recall times in your life when you simply had to endure hardship—even deep losses—because of love.

2. In our earthly lives, the Bible does not give us spiritual escapes to heavenly bliss, but we are called and sent into the world as God's chosen ones. The promise of heaven on earth awaits the Lord's return. When Peter proposed building three "dwellings" on the mountain, perhaps he was thinking of the shelters the Israelites built on their journey through the wilderness. The Jewish festival of "tabernacles" or "booths" is still celebrated in remembrance of God's deliverance. Maybe Peter wasn't wrong, although Luke reports that Peter made that suggestion, "not knowing what he said" (9:33).

• Tell of a time when you have "come down to earth" from "a mountaintop experience" or spiritual high point in your life. How did you see your daily life differently from that moment on?

Wrap–up

Be ready to look back over the work the group has done during the session.

Pray

How good, Lord, to be here! Your beauty to behold
where Moses and Elijah stand, your messengers of old.
Fulfiller of the past and hope of things to be,
we hail your body glorified and our redemption see.
How good, Lord, to be here! Yet we may not remain;
but since you bid us leave the mount, come with us to the plain.
Amen.
("How Good, Lord, to Be Here!" ELW 315, verses 2, 3, 5)

Extending the Conversation

Homework

1. Read the next session's Bible text: Luke 15:1–32.

2. For a glimpse of Jesus' determination to accomplish his mission, read Luke 9:51–62. This is the major turning point in the story following the transfiguration when Jesus "turns his face" and sets his course toward Jerusalem. We already know from his passion predictions (Luke 9:22, 44), that he will be moving into grave danger and death and that those who follow him will share those hazards. Jesus is enacting the prophetic script to "set his face" (Isaiah

50:7; Ezekiel 21:1–2). The confrontation of God's will versus human willfulness lies ahead.

3. Notice in Luke 13:31–35 how Jesus refuses to let some Pharisees (who probably meant well) to protect him from Herod's threats. Although he regularly turns aside to help people in need, Jesus will not be deterred from his mission on his journey to Jerusalem (19:41–44).

Enrichment

1. If you wish to read through the entire book of Luke during this unit, read the following sections this week.

Day 1: Luke 9:37–62

Day 2: Luke 10:1–24

Day 3: Luke 10:25–11:13

Day 4: Luke 11:14–54

Day 5: Luke 12:1–59

Day 6: Luke 13:1–35

Day 7: Luke 14:1–35

2. When we confess that Jesus was "sacrificed for our sins," we may be thinking about how lambs were sacrificed in the temple and their blood was "poured out." Mark's Gospel (10:45) speaks that way when Jesus tells his disciples that the Son of Man came to give "to give his life a ransom for many." Luke uses very few of the words from the priestly tradition of temple sacrifice, instead describing the conflict with Jesus' adversaries as unavoidable—even necessary—because God intends to rule in mercy and justice. This is the prophetic tradition of God's reign in human history. The prophetic witness understands why it was necessary for Jesus to die in terms of God's conflict against the forces that oppose God. Those include people who are set against God (i.e., sin), human principalities protecting their powers (e.g., the Roman and Jewish rulers), and the forces of evil (e.g., the demons).

- Write and act out a script of someone who made the "ultimate sacrifice" so that others might live. This might be the story of someone who gave up his or her place in a lifeboat so children would survive, or a soldier who took enemy fire so the others in the squad could find cover.

- Next, think about how Jesus put himself in harm's way, even knowing that he would die, for your liberation from death. The apostle Paul thought deeply about why Jesus had to die in just such terms—to prove God's love for us: "God proves [God's] love for us in that while we were still sinners Christ died for us" (Romans 5:8).

 Notes

Notes

For Further Reading

The Gospel According to Luke by Michael Patella in New Collegeville Bible Commentary Series (Collegeville, MN: Liturgical Press, 2005), pp. 63–67.

"Session 5: Jesus Enacts Scripture" in *Learning Luke: The Apostolic Gospel* by David L. Tiede and friends (selectlearning.org).

Provoking the Gospel of Luke: A Storyteller's Commentary by Richard W. Swanson (Cleveland: Pilgrim Press, 2006). pp. 109–112.

Augsburg Commentary on the New Testament: Luke by David L. Tiede (Minneapolis: Augsburg Fortress, 1988), pp. 181–191.

Luke 15:1–32

Learner
Session
Guide

Focus Statement

Just when we may be tempted to resent the way Jesus includes people who are not worthy, he invites us to join the rollicking joy in heaven over the return of the lost.

Key Verse

While he was still far off, his father saw him and was filled with compassion; he ran and put his arms around him and kissed him. Luke 15:20

And Grace Will Lead Me Home

Focus Image

Return of the Prodigal Son
Rembrandt Harmensz van Rijn (1606–1669 Dutch)
State Hermitage Museum, St. Petersburg, Russia
© SuperStock / SuperStock

Gather

Check-in

Take this time to connect or reconnect with the others in your group. Be ready to share new thoughts or insights about your last session.

Pray

Heavenly Father, we thank you that you are more ready to welcome our return than we are to come to you. We admit that our pride tempts us to be self-righteous, even resentful, when your compassion extends to people we regard as unworthy. But when we are the ones whom you welcome while we are still far off, or when someone we love returns home, we join the angels in heaven in praising your amazing grace. Open now our hearts and minds to learn the ways of your compassion and to rejoice in Jesus' love. Amen.

Focus Activity

Take a quiet moment to recall a time in your own life when someone loved you, even though you did not deserve it. Maybe it was a teacher or a parent or grandparent or a friend who stood by

Notes

you when others were disapproving. If you could thank that person today, what would you say? How did such love empower you to care for someone else?

Open Scripture

Read Luke 15:1–32.

- What caught your attention when you heard these three stories read together?

- Are any of the characters in the stories unreasonable or even unfair?

- Did you learn anything surprising about God in these familiar stories? If so, what?

Join the Conversation

Literary Context

1. All three of the stories in Luke 15 are popular and beloved, even by people who have never read Luke's Gospel. Taken together, all three stories in Luke 15 explore what Jesus revealed in Luke 14 about the hospitality of God's kingdom, rejecting standard protocols for banqueting with the elect and the elite. Luke also introduces these stories as Jesus' direct response to the criticism of the Pharisees and the scribes in 15:2—"This fellow welcomes sinners and eats with them."

- What common theme or themes do you see connecting these stories in Luke 15?

- Think about the characters in each of the stories. What motivates them to do what they do? Which character surprised you the most? Why? With which character do you most identify? Why?

2. Every grade school child knows how it feels to be included or excluded from a birthday party, and adults are also quick to look for their own names on guest lists. Those who are "chosen" are the "elect," and the others often feel unworthy.

Notes

- Whom does Jesus invite to the table in the story in Luke 14:7–14? What parallel do you see between that story and the stories in Luke 15?

- Make a guest list for your church's next anniversary. What would the church be like—what would our lives be like—if we followed Jesus' counsel to his host in Luke 14:12–14?

3. Attempts to interpret Jesus' parables as morality stories, like Aesop's fables, stumble over obvious realities. The shepherd was not prudent in leaving 99 sheep in the wilderness. The woman was obsessed with finding a small coin to the point that her party for her neighbors probably cost more than the coin was worth.

- What about the younger son (the prodigal)? What seems obvious about what he deserves?

- And what about the older son, the prodigal's brother? Is his reaction expected or not? Why?

- Look again at the older son's speech in 15:29–30. Put the elder son's words in the context of the grumbling from the Pharisees and the scribes about Jesus: "This fellow welcomes sinners and eats with them" (Luke 15:2). What similarities do you see?

Historical Context

These little stories, or parables, are powerful all by themselves, but their force is felt even more deeply in the context that Jesus told them. Consider both the immediate context of the criticism from the Pharisees and the larger realm of the Roman Order. You don't need to be an expert in Jewish or Roman history to sense similarities to our own times.

Notes

Christ and the Pharisees by Edward Armitage (1817–1896 British)
© SuperStock / SuperStock

1. Who were the Pharisees? The Pharisees were not bad people. In modern times, non–Jewish Christians often use the word "Pharisee" as an insult to or about people they regard as rigid and self–righteous. It is important to remember that according to Luke, Jesus dined in the house of a Pharisee at least twice (Luke 7:36–50; 11:37–41), and some of the believers in Acts are identified as belonging "to the sect of the Pharisees" (Acts 15:5). Yes, these stories are marked with tension over whether the Pharisees could accept Jesus' remarkable acceptance of outsiders, but Luke presents Jesus as a teacher among the Pharisees and reminds us that some of the Pharisees belonged to the "believers." These Pharisees were not adversaries, but followers of Jesus.

• Look at the piece of art above entitled *Christ and the Pharisees*. Most art that depicts Jesus and the Pharisees shows the biblical scenes when they are in conflict. What strikes you about this scene? Do you think of Jesus as being a teacher "among" the Pharisees? How (if at all) does that affect the way you think of the relationship between Jesus and the Pharisees?

2. "The Pharisees and the scribes" worked together to renew Israel's faithfulness to God. The scriptures were copied by the scribes to be circulated in the synagogues. Those of us who are writing these materials for the Book of Faith initiative are modern scribes. The Pharisees were members of a reform movement, calling Israel to obedience to God's law. Some of them criticized the way that certain high priests collaborated with the Greek or Roman occupation forces to keep their positions or abused their office for personal gain. Some Pharisees were crucified by the tyrants. The Pharisees also taught the people how to keep their homes and their synagogues purified according to God's law.

- Have you ever considered the positive contribution that the Pharisees and scribes made to Jewish life and faith? Why or why not?

- It is easy to criticize the Pharisees, but what if they are like your neighbors or like you? They were striving to do the right thing, but they were tempted to be more judgmental than compassionate! Why is it easy to judge others but more difficult to walk in another's shoes?

3. What about modern Christian Pharisees? There is an old joke about a person who objected to serving wine at communion. The pastor observed, "Yes, but Jesus drank wine." "Oh, I know that," said the objector, "but that's the one thing I don't like about Jesus!" Give the Pharisees a break. Consider these stories from their point of view, or from the elder brother's point of view. Write a paragraph that expresses their reasonable objection. What is "the one thing you don't like about Jesus" if you are one of the "ninety-nine righteous persons who need no repentance" (Luke 15:7)?

4. Consider Jesus from the point of view of the Roman occupation forces. The Roman world was run by "Law and Order!"; generally, it was well run, but there was also a dark side to Roman systems of discipline and control. This harsher view will be evident in Session 7 on Jesus' trial and execution. Imagine a scene in Herod's court or in Pilate's palace. In Luke 9:9, Herod was already musing, "John I beheaded; but who is this about whom I hear such things?" And Jesus already mentioned Pilate as the tyrant who mixed the blood of the Galileans with their sacrifices (Luke 13:1). The Pharisees are the ones who warned Jesus, "Herod wants to kill you" (13:31).

- Imagine that you are Herod or Pilate and you have heard rumors, maybe inaccurate stories, about a prophet-teacher who is traveling the countryside, announcing God's reign of compassion, love for the unworthy, and acceptance of outsiders. Why would you want that prophet-teacher out of the way?

Lutheran Context

1. The Lutheran confession of the gospel is an invitation to saving trust in God's love. "While we were still sinners Christ died for us," declared Paul (Romans 5:8). "For by grace you have been saved through faith, and this is not your own doing; it is the gift of God" (Ephesians 2:8). Where do you see this "gospel" message played out in the story of the prodigal?

2. The elder son was religiously righteous. He probably would have been more concerned with protecting the ninety-nine sheep who had

Notes

Notes

not strayed and less impressed by the extravagant preoccupation by the shepherd or the woman about the one that was lost.

- Do you think the elder brother believed his younger brother's confession, "Father, I have sinned against heaven and before you. I am no longer worthy to be called your son," or do you think he suspected that the younger brother was still manipulating the situation? Why or why not?

- If it is true that "while we were still sinners Christ died for us," does it matter whether the elder son has read his brother correctly or if the younger son's return/repentance was truly genuine? Why or why not? From a "gospel perspective," what does matter?

3. Imagine the parable of the prodigal in a modern setting. For example, consider a loving parent who lavishes time and resources on a child who is in trouble with himself/herself, the law, and the world. How many times will the "lost one" go to rehab? And what is a sober, responsible sibling going to think? Even when a parent's searching and abundant love is not able to rescue the lost, this "amazing grace" is a human enactment of God's compassion. Have you experienced or seen examples of such "grace–filled" love and compassion?

Devotional Context

1. These stories reveal the deep mystery of the joy of heaven in recovering the lost. The compassion of the father is more than the wayward son can expect, and his extravagant love can hardly be grasped or tolerated by the righteous son. Freed from self–righteousness, the faithful relinquish their right to envy God's reception of the wayward. "How blessed are those who know their need of God." Only forgiven sinners stand at the foot of the cross.

- When have you acted like the younger brother, the older brother, or the father?

- Who are the lost, those who want or need to be welcomed home?

2. Take a walk into the chancel of your church. Who is welcome at the Lord's table (Holy Communion) in your congregation? Who decides who is welcome, and do all agree with these procedures or policies? What, if anything, might you change? Why? Do you think it pleases God when sinners join Jesus' meal? Do you think it is responsible to insist on some moral standards, some observance of God's law, or some evidence of true repentance for admission to the table?

3. Look at the Focus Image once again. After what you have read and discussed, what other titles might you give to this painting? Why?

4. What prayer or prayers do these stories prompt for you?

Wrap-up

Be ready to look back over the work your group has done in this session.

Pray

God of compassion, you welcome the wayward, and you embrace all with your mercy. By our baptism clothe us with garments of your grace, and feed us at the table of your love, through Jesus Christ, our Savior and Lord, who lives and reigns with you and the Holy Spirit, one God, now and forever. Amen.
(Prayer for Fourth Sunday in Lent, Year C, ELW, p. 28)

Extending the Conversation

Homework

1. Read the next session's Bible text: Luke 23:26–49.

2. The Gospel story reveals not only the extravagance of God's love but also its cost. As you read the chapters in Luke prior to the next meeting of the Book of Faith group, make a list of the places where Jesus knows 1) what this mission of love will cost him and 2) how costly it will be for Jesus' followers in the mission ahead.

3. Pay a visit to one of the older saints in your congregation or a couple who have been married for decades. Ask them to tell you about when their love was tested in sorrow or brokenness. What price did they or someone pay because "that's what you do when you love someone?" How were they assured of God's love for them through the dark time?

Enrichment

1. If you wish to read through the entire book of Luke during this unit, read the following sections this week.

    Day 1: Luke 16:1–31

    Day 2: Luke 17:1–37

    Day 3: Luke 18:1–30

    Day 4: Luke 18:31–19:10

    Day 5: Luke 19:11–47

    Day 6: Luke 20:1–26

    Day 7: Luke 20:27–47

2. In this session, Jesus' parables are revelations of God's gracious reign, not mere lessons in behavior. Many Bible dictionaries have good, brief introductions to the interpretation of Jesus' parables as the "riddles" or "revelations" of God's reign. Some interpreters have argued that our understanding of Jesus' parables has been distorted

 Notes

Notes

by moralizing their messages, thereby missing the mystery of God that they disclose.

- Read one or more of the brief Bible dictionary articles on "parables" and alert the group to the ways that Jesus surprised his listeners in each of these parables.

- When Jesus tells of the love of the father, he is echoing the witness of Israel's prophets to God's compassion, even God's pathos, or suffering, when the people have lost their way. Read Ezekiel 34, for example, to hear God's anguish as well as God's commitment to bring the people—not just an individual—to safety: "I myself will search for my sheep, and will seek them out."

For Further Reading

The Gospel According to Luke by Michael Patella in New Collegeville Bible Commentary Series (Collegeville, MN: Liturgical Press, 2005), pp. 102–107.

"Session 7: "Parables and Revelation" in *Learning Luke: The Apostolic Gospel* by David L. Tiede and friends (selectlearning.org).

Provoking the Gospel of Luke: A Storyteller's Commentary by Richard W. Swanson (Cleveland: Pilgrim Press, 2006), pp. 128–134, 193–198.

Augsburg Commentary on the New Testament: Luke by David L. Tiede (Minneapolis: Augsburg Fortress, 1988), pp. 272–281.

Luke 23:26–49

Learner Session Guide

Focus Statement

The execution of Jesus tested all of God's promises of justice and mercy. Standing at the foot of the cross, we are both tormented and deeply inspired by what we see and hear.

Key Verse

When the centurion saw what had taken place, he praised God and said, "Certainly this man was innocent."
Luke 23:47

Ah, Holy Jesus, How Hast Thou Offended?

 Focus Image

Pardoning of the Penitent Thief
James Tissot (1836–1902/French)
© SuperStock / SuperStock

Gather

Check–in

Take this time to connect or reconnect with the others in your group. Be ready to share new thoughts or insights about your last session.

Pray

Almighty God, look with loving mercy on your family, for whom our Lord Jesus Christ was willing to be betrayed, to be given over to the hands of sinners, and to suffer death on the cross; who now lives and reigns with you and the Holy Spirit, one God, forever and ever. Amen.
(Collect for Good Friday, ELW, p. 31)

Focus Activity

Remember a time when you experienced how unfair life can be. Maybe it was something that was done to you. Maybe you watched as others were mean or even brutal to a childhood friend or a vulnerable person. Maybe it was a wartime experience. Maybe you participated in ways you now regret. Then remember Jesus' own

Notes

innocent suffering. Write a confidential prayer, calling God to forgive and care for all who suffer.

Open Scripture

Read Luke 23:26-49.

- What do you find most troubling about this story of Jesus' execution?

- What would you have thought if you walked in on this crucifixion from somewhere else without knowing what was happening?

- What words or actions by the people described in this passage surprise you the most?

Join the Conversation

Literary Context

1. Luke carefully identifies the differing roles of all who are present at Jesus' execution. Look at the Focus Image for this session. What characters can you identify based on Luke's depiction of the crucifixion?

- What "attitude" is displayed toward Jesus by the Roman soldiers, Jewish leaders, and the first criminal?

- Recite aloud the derisive comments of the leaders (verse 35), the soldiers (verses 36–37), and the first criminal (verse 39), first in their evil tone of voice.

2. Notice the sign that is put above Jesus' head on the cross: "This is the King of the Jews" (23:38). The political point of the execution was to warn against any who would dare to claim non-Roman authority to rule. But we know that their sarcastic threats actually tell the truth. How could the sarcastic and mocking statements in verses 35–39 be turned into confessions of faith?

3. The Roman centurion's words stand in contrast to the mocking earlier in the scene. The centurion "saw what had taken place" with the eyes of faith. Recite verse 47 with particular care for how he declares Jesus "innocent." This word could also be translated as "righteous." Whatever the centurion meant to say, (see also Mark

15:39, "God's Son"), the early Christians understood his declaration as identifying Jesus as God's promised "Righteous One" (Acts 3:14; 7:52; 22:14).

- What significance do you see in the words of the centurion, who was supposed to swear allegiance to the emperor?

- What about those who "returned home, beating their breasts" (23:48)? You might be helped to know that the word in Greek for "returned home" is literally "they turned" or even "they repented." What do you suppose they were saying to themselves about what they had just seen and heard as they turned away to go home?

Historical Context

1. Every Sunday when we recite the Apostles' Creed in worship, we remember that Jesus Christ was "crucified under Pontius Pilate." Jesus was his given name, and Christ means Messiah or "anointed one." In Israel, the kings were not crowned, but like King David, Jesus was anointed on divine authority with the Holy Spirit and with power (see 1 Samuel 16; Psalm 2; Acts 10:38).

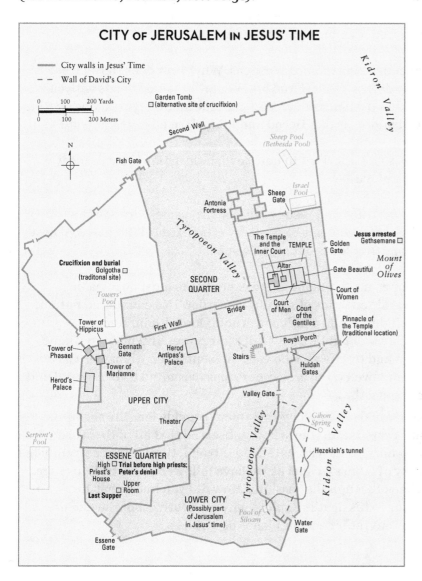

CITY OF JERUSALEM IN JESUS' TIME

Notes

Read Luke 23:1–12. Keep in mind that both the Roman procurator Pontius Pilate and Herod Antipas were in Jerusalem only because of the Passover.

- Look at the map on page 51\ and note key locations mentioned in the trials and crucifixion of Jesus. Pilate most likely headquartered at the Fortress Antonia. Jesus was arrested in the Garden of Gethsemane, taken to the High Priest's house, and then shuttled back and forth between Pilate and Herod Antipas before going to the cross on Golgotha.

- What were the charges against Jesus that might have provoked the Roman procurator, Pontius Pilate? What question does Pilate ask Jesus? How does Jesus answer? What does Pilate conclude from this answer?

- The Roman Senate named Herod the Great "The King of the Jews" (see Matthew 2:1), and Caesar Augustus (see Luke 2) gave him authority to rule in Judea and Galilee. His sons were not given this title, but Herod Antipas, who appears in Luke's story, yearned to be named "King of the Jews," provoking animosity with Pilate, the Roman procurator (see Luke 23:12). Based on that, why do you think this question was important to Pilate?

2. Pilate sends Jesus to Herod Antipas. Why? How does Herod treat Jesus? Why do you think Herod and Pilate "became friends with each other" on that particular day? How genuine and/or cynical do you think the "friendship" was that Herod and Pilate formed in Jesus' trial?

3. Why it is still important to non–Jewish Christians that Jesus was truly "King of the Jews"?

4. If Pilate does not find Jesus guilty of any crime, why does he eventually sentence Jesus to death by crucifixion? Who had the most to gain by getting Jesus out of the way?

5. The Romans used crucifixion to execute the most despicable criminals and "enemies of the Roman Order." No conquered nation, including Judea, could conduct a crucifixion without Roman authority. It was a public display of their power, intended to shame the victims and terrify all who were present. Even when worn as an ornament or jewelry, the cross continues to remind us of a brutal and humiliating death.

- All four Gospels in the New Testament provide lengthy accounts of Jesus' crucifixion. One scholar observed that all of them are "passion narratives with extended introductions." That certainly fits our study of Luke's Gospel as we have followed Jesus to Jerusalem. Think back through the sessions. How did you know that Jesus was on his way to his death? Explore why his death is not the end of his ministry, but rather accomplishes or fulfills it.

Lutheran Context

1. Martin Luther taught the "theology of the cross," emphasizing both the dire reality of Jesus' gruesome death and the profound salvation that God accomplished through it. The "theology of the cross" is strong medicine for us and our human condition. The media often create public excitement about "The Gospel of Thomas" or some "newly discovered" Gnostic gospel. Almost none of those accounts, even from early centuries, pays attention to Jesus' crucifixion. Some even deny that it happened. Those other gospels may provide winsome wisdom from Jesus as a teacher, but compared to the biblical "theology of the cross," they are only mild cures for mild diseases.

- How is Jesus' death the ultimate revelation of God's profound salvation for us?
- Why is the cross so important to our understanding of Jesus' mission?

2. In his explanation to the second article of the Apostles' Creed in the Small Catechism, Luther says the following about Jesus:

He has redeemed me, a lost and condemned human being. He has purchased and freed me from all sins, from death, and from the power of the devil, not with gold or silver but with his holy, precious blood and with his innocent suffering and death. He has done all this in order that I may belong to him, live under him in his kingdom, and serve him in eternal righteousness, innocence, and blessedness, just as he is risen from the dead and lives and rules eternally.

- What stands out to you in these words?
- Without the cross, would these words be "true"? Why or why not?

Devotional Context

1. You need to read all four Gospels to see how each evangelist highlights one or more of Jesus' "seven last words" from the cross. Luke reports three of these words at very critical points in our story (Luke 23:34, 43, 46). Note that the first "word" (verse 34) is generally printed in brackets in our Bibles because several ancient Greek copies or manuscripts did not include it, and the narrative flows smoothly without quoting Jesus. What Jesus is quoted as saying, however, fits deeply with Luke's testimony, and some scholars propose that this "word" was dropped by Gentile anti-Jewish scribes who doubted God's forgiveness for Jesus' executioners, or even for all Jews.

Listen to hear each of these words, as if you are standing at the foot of the cross.

 Notes

Notes

- The first is the word of forgiveness (verse 34), spoken during the cruel, inhuman execution. How does Jesus' bond with the Father focus his mission of love? Also listen to Jesus' prayer to God on the Mount of Olives in Luke 22:42. Where has the depth of such forgiveness touched your life, your family, or your congregation?

- The second word (verse 43) is the granting of God's promise of paradise to an unworthy criminal who trusts Jesus as both are in the throes of dying. Where have you seen such unlikely faith? How strong is Christ Jesus to speak comfort during his own suffering?

- The third word (verse 46) is rich in the faith that Jesus is enveloped in God's Spirit. In Greek, the word for "spirit" is *pneuma*—like the word for the breath of our lungs or the pneumatic air in our tires—and the same word is used in Greek for saying, "he breathed his last." So Jesus returned the breath of God and then breathed his last, or gave his "spirit" to God and then "expired." Here is the unity of Jesus with God in "spirit," in purpose, in love, embodied in Jesus' life and breath as a mortal human. What do you think of the idea that Jesus gave his "spirit" to God? How does that relate to his mission?

2. When Jesus later sends the "Holy Spirit" upon the church, it is God's powerful Breath (Acts 1:4–5, 8; 2:1–4). Describe a time when you saw "the breath of life" animate someone in peril or when a dear one returned their breath to God as they "expired."

3. Through the centuries, believers have learned that the best way to testify to what God was doing in Jesus' death is not to "explain it" as if we could read God's mind, but to join the centurion in "praising God" for a wonder too deep to understand with mortal reason.

- Read Philippians 2:5–11. This may be the earliest Christian hymn we still have in praise of the "mind that was in Christ Jesus," confident that Jesus is truly enacting God's way of ruling in heaven and on earth. What strikes you about these words? What might it have to say about being a follower of Jesus?

Wrap-up

Be ready to look back over the work your group has done in this session.

Pray

To sustain Luke's witness to the anguish and hope of Jesus' death, pray or sing the great hymn for Holy Week, "Ah, Holy Jesus" (ELW 349):

Ah, holy Jesus, how hast thou offended that we to judge thee have in hate pretended? By foes derided, by thine own rejected, O most afflicted.

Who was the guilty? Who brought this upon thee? Alas, my treason, Jesus, hath undone thee. 'Twas I, Lord Jesus, I it was denied thee; I crucified thee.

Lo, the Good Shepherd for the sheep is offered; the slave hath sinned, and the Son hath suffered; for our atonement, while we nothing heeded, God interceded.

For me, kind Jesus, was thine incarnation, thy mortal sorrow, and thy life's oblation; thy death of anguish and thy bitter passion, for my salvation.

Therefore, kind Jesus, since I cannot pay thee, I do adore thee, and will every pray thee; think on thy pity and thy love unswerving, not my deserving.
Amen.

Extending the Conversation

Homework

1. Read the next session's Bible text: Luke 24:13–35.

2. Place a cross on your nightstand during the coming week, then recite each of Jesus' last words as Luke reported them, listening for God's promises to you:

"Father, forgive them; for they do not know what they are doing!"

"Truly I tell you, today you will be with me in Paradise."

"Father, into your hands I commend my spirit."

3. Do some research on the lives of Herod Antipas and Pontius Pilate. Report your findings to the class next week.

 Notes

Notes

Enrichment

1. If you wish to read through the entire book of Luke during this unit, read the following sections this week.

Day 1: Luke 21:1–19

Day 2: Luke 21:20–36

Day 3: Luke 21:37–22:13

Day 4: Luke 22:14–34

Day 5: Luke 22:35–53

Day 6: Luke 22:54–71

Day 7: Luke 23:1–25

2. In session 5, we explored Jesus' transfiguration on the mountain and discussed the "exodus" or "departure" that Jesus "was about to accomplish at Jerusalem" (Luke 9:31). During your reading this week of Luke 22:1–34 (days 3 and 4 on the schedule above), remember the Passover as the story of Israel's exodus from slavery.

• How did Jesus accomplish a new liberation for all people?

• How is Judas' betrayal of Jesus (Luke 22:3–6, 47–48) different from Peter's denial (Luke 22:54-62)? Have you ever been betrayed? Have you ever denied your faith in Jesus? How does Jesus' love for Peter give you hope?

3. All Christians must be reminded that Jesus was a Jew, his people were Jewish, and all the characters in the story (except the Romans) are Jewish. Like many prophetic voices in Israel's history, Jesus and the evangelist call Israel to repentance (see also Peter in Acts 2:22–36). But all of God's people, including Peter and the disciples, were complicit in Jesus' death, and as Peter proclaimed in Acts 2:39, "the promise is for you, for your children, and for all who are far away, everyone whom the Lord our God calls to him." Someone may wish to investigate the rich discussion among scholars about how this Jewish story eventually was misinterpreted as anti-Jewish or anti-Semitic.

For Further Reading

The Gospel According to Luke by Michael Patella in New Collegeville Bible Commentary Series (Collegeville, MN: Liturgical Press, 2005), pp. 147–152.

"Session 11: The King of the Jews" in *Learning Luke: The Apostolic Gospel* by David L. Tiede and friends (selectlearning.org).

Provoking the Gospel of Luke: A Storyteller's Commentary by Richard W. Swanson (Cleveland: Pilgrim Press, 2006), pp. 128–139.

Augsburg Commentary on the New Testament: Luke by David L. Tiede (Minneapolis: Augsburg Fortress, 1988), pp. 411–427.

Learner Session Guide

Focus Statement

The world is changed in the light of Jesus' resurrection. Israel's Scriptures testify from the past. The new age of the resurrection of the righteous has dawned in the present. The future is now the arena for the repentance and forgiveness of all the nations.

Key Verse

They said to each other, "Were not our hearts burning within us while he was talking to us on the road, while he was opening the scriptures to us?"
Luke 24:32

How Did Jesus' Resurrection Change the World?

 Focus Image

© SoFood / SuperStock

Gather

Check-in

Take this time to connect or reconnect with the others in your group. Be ready to share new thoughts or insights about your last session.

Pray

O God, whose blessed Son made himself known to his disciples in the breaking of bread, open the eyes of our faith, that we may behold him in all his redeeming work, Jesus Christ, our Savior and Lord, who lives and reigns with you and the Holy Spirit, one God, now and forever. Amen.
(Prayer for the evening of Easter Day, ELW, p. 32)

Focus Activity

Share with at least one other person what you recall to be one of the most memorable meals you ever had. What made it memorable? Was it the food, the person or people you were with, the purpose for the meal, or something that happened during the meal?

Notes

Read Luke 24:13-35.

- What images or words stood out for you in this story?

- What was surprising or confusing?

- Why do you think Luke tells this particular story?

Join the Conversation

Literary Context

1. This story is another literary masterpiece from the writer of Luke. None of the other Gospels mentions these events, but the risen Jesus also gave bread and fish to his disciples by the shore in John's Gospel (John 21:9-13). Compare this story in Luke to John's story. What similarities do you see?

2. Luke's story draws us deeply into the mystery of why people are often so blind to what is truly happening. This human reality is also commonly depicted in tragic dramas when someone fails to see what is obvious to the audience.

- The two followers don't recognize Jesus at first. How does that fact add to the impact of the end of the story?

3. The prophets of Israel often spoke of the "spiritual blindness" of God's people. They saw that blindness as a sign of human self-absorption. In this story in Luke, the risen Messiah teaches his disciples how God is at work in what is happening, whether people see it or not. The word "disciples" literally means "learners." Notice that Jesus teaches his followers/learners from "Moses and all the prophets" even before they recognize who he is. We know that "Jesus

himself" is walking with them (verse 15), but they don't recognize him; in fact, they can't because "their eyes were kept from recognizing him" (verse 16). They only recognize him for who he is when "their eyes were opened" (verse 31) and as he "took bread, blessed and broke it, and gave it to them" (verse 30).

• How do you feel when it says, "Their eyes were kept from recognizing him"? What or who do you imagine prevented their recognition of Jesus?

• What or who "opened their eyes"?

4. When the scriptures are read regularly in public worship, they often seem routine, but sometimes we are touched in ways we had not expected. Recalling what they felt before they knew it was Jesus, these disciples, "said to each other, 'Were not our hearts burning within us while he was talking to us on the road, while he was opening the scriptures to us?'" When John Wesley heard a reading of Luther's commentary on Galatians, his heart was "strangely warmed" in awareness of God's unexpected presence. Has that ever happened to you or to someone you know?

Historical Context

1. Take a look at the map "Palestine in Jesus' Time" on p. 8. Notice how close Emmaus was to Jerusalem. What do you suppose the people in Jerusalem and the surrounding area were saying about the events related to Jesus' death? What does Cleopas' question (24:18) seem to imply?

2. Jesus' resurrection is both an historical event (because it happened at a specific time in human history) and a disruption when God's future broke into human history. When the widow's son at Nain was revived from death, the people declared, "A great prophet has risen among us!" and "God has looked favorably on his people" (Luke 7:16). The young man probably went back to his life when "Jesus gave him to his mother" (7:15). But Jesus' resurrection was an event that changed the world, marking the fulfillment of all of Israel's history and the dawn of God's apostolic mission of the church.

• How is this story from Luke a glimpse into a world where everything has changed? Notice the wonder and confusion of the people who were still disappointed, afraid, and awed.

• If local newspapers had existed, do you think Jesus' death would have been front-page news? Why or why not?

Notes

3. A second historical context for this story is the time when Luke wrote his "orderly account of the events that have been fulfilled among us" (Luke 1:1) sometime in the late first century, probably about fifty years or so after Jesus' resurrection. About forty years after Jesus' resurrection, the Romans destroyed the temple in Jerusalem during a Jewish uprising.

• How do you suppose this story sounded to Jesus' followers after the Romans had destroyed the temple, Israel was scattered, and the Jesus movement was expanding?

4. Notice how thoroughly the story is filled with Israel's Scriptures, what Christians refer to as the "Old Testament." It's important to remember that Jesus' scriptures were scriptures of Israel.

• Imagine you are a Christian preacher in Rome. If you picked up and expanded upon Jesus' own words, "Then beginning with Moses and all the prophets, he interpreted to them the things about himself in all the scriptures" (24:27), what would you say?

Lutheran Context

1. Using the principle of scripture interpreting scripture, explore how the resurrection is described in the following passages. How do these passages shed light on the meaning of the resurrected Jesus?

• John 11:17–27
• 1 Corinthians 15:12–23

2. Jesus' followers recognized Jesus when he broke bread and gave it to them (Luke 24:30). Think about how the Lord's Supper, Holy Communion, is celebrated in worship in your church.

• How would you compare the sharing of bread, Christ's body, in the sacrament to what happened in the meal Jesus shared with the two followers?

• Think about the people who visit your congregation at Easter. Maybe they come for family events or because they hope to hear a word of hope. The music and flowers are lovely. You are now among Jesus' disciples who know that he is alive. How can you and your congregation be his "apostles" to the visitors, recognizing the presence of the living Lord in the opening of the scriptures and the breaking of bread?

3. The Lutheran tradition specializes in thanksgiving for the forgiveness of sins and in trusting God's calling of all Christians in their homes and families, their public lives, their paid and unpaid work, and their communities of worship. At the close of worship, the

pastor routinely says, "Go in peace. Serve the Lord!" and the people respond, "Thanks be to God!"

- Since Jesus is risen from the dead, it is time to ask each other, "How is that part about 'serving the Lord' going for you?"

Devotional Context

1. We talked about two different historical "contexts" for understanding the story. A third historical context is the "here and now." Jesus not only came back from the dead, but he has also been vindicated as God's true Messiah and Lord of heaven and earth for all time and eternity. Jesus also continues to make himself known to us in his Word and in the breaking of bread of the Lord's Supper.

- As you go into your life in the world, including your places of work and play, what difference does it make that Jesus died and God raised him from the dead?
- What helps you to recognize God at work in your life and to see Jesus for who he is?

2. Look again at the Focus Image for this session. What do you see? Who is the person holding the bread? What's his "story"? How has Jesus been made known to you in the breaking of bread?

3. Describe a time when you had a rich, spiritual conversation with a stranger. Maybe you even discussed your hopes and disappointments as you felt drawn to say things or ready to hear things you had not discussed with anyone. Maybe it was on a plane or at a camp or cruise where you were traveling together without previously knowing each other. As you listen in on the conversation of these travelers on the road to Emmaus, do you recall times when you experienced God's unexpected presence among strangers?

4. Jesus' resurrection shines God's light of promise into all of life because death is no longer ultimate. If you read the prayers in the Service of Christian Burial, you will notice how realistic Christian funerals are about the decay of the mortal body. But they also rejoice in the confidence in the sure and certain hope of the resurrection.

- What person do you know, or have you known, who is the best example of one who lives in the sure and certain hope of the resurrection?

Wrap-up

Be ready to look back over the work your group has done in this session.

 Notes

Notes

Pray

Lord Jesus, we journey with your disciples in awe and wonder at your resurrection. You have been vindicated as Messiah, Lord, and Savior, for us and for the world. Open the eyes of our hearts, Lord, to recognize you among us in your word, in the opening of the Scriptures, and in the breaking of bread. We thank you for our bodies, and we praise you that we are already enfolded in the life of your resurrected body until the time we are raised from the dead ourselves. In you, we catch a glimpse of the world to come, but we rejoice here and now to be sent as your people into this world you so love. In your holy name, we pray. Amen.

Extending the Conversation

Homework

1. Consider going back over parts of Luke's Gospel that were not covered in this study. Use what you have learned in this course to "inform" your own study and reading of Luke.

2. What part of the Bible would you like to know more about? Give some thought to what you might like to read or study next.

Enrichment

1. Luke's story of Jesus reaches a crescendo in his resurrection, but it does not stop there because God is not done with the world. Read the rest of Luke 24 and continue on in the Acts of the Apostles to see how Jesus' resurrection paves the way for the Holy Spirit to empower the church in God's continuing mission of promise and hope for all. Notice in Peter's sermon on Pentecost that the pouring out of the Spirit is a sign of the fulfillment of God's scriptural promise of an inspired people and the opening of the doors of salvation to "everyone who calls on the name of the Lord" (Acts 2:14–21). Notice also how Peter's announcement of the resurrection of the crucified Messiah first strikes fear in the people, "What shall we do?" But Jesus' resurrection is an invitation to return to God (repent) with baptism, "for the promise is for you, for your children, and for all who are far away, everyone whom the Lord our God calls to him." (Acts 2:36–39). If you wish to complete your reading of the entire book of Luke and see how it flows into its sequel, The Acts of the Apostles, read the following sections this week.

Day 1: Luke 24:1–12

Day 2: Luke 24:36–41

Day 3: Luke 24:44–53

Day 4: Acts 1:1–11

Day 5: Acts 1:12–26

Day 6: Acts 2:1–21

Day 7: Acts 2:22–47

 Notes

2. Interview a nurse or physician about how his or her care of people expresses God's love for human bodies, including the tender care for those who are dying in hospice. Christian ministries of healing have always trusted God's love for the body without pretending that mortal humans will live forever. Offer prayers of thanksgiving for those who care for the sick, the elderly, and the dying.

For Further Reading

The Gospel According to Luke by Michael Patella in New Collegeville Bible Commentary Series (Collegeville, MN: Liturgical Press, 2005), pp. 153–158.

"Session 12: Crucified and Raised" in *Learning Luke: The Apostolic Gospel* by David L. Tiede and friends (selectlearning.org).

Provoking the Gospel of Luke: A Storyteller's Commentary by Richard W. Swanson (Cleveland: Pilgrim Press, 2006), pp. 139–146.

Augsburg Commentary on the New Testament: Luke by David L. Tiede (Minneapolis: Augsburg Fortress, 1988), pp. 432–444.

CPSIA information can be obtained
at www.ICGtesting.com
Printed in the USA
LVHW062122160222
711351LV00004B/7